Common Core Lessons & Activities:
Space Science

By Carole Marsh

Published by Gallopade International, Inc.

Printed in the U.S.A. (Peachtree City, Georgia)

TABLE OF CONTENTS

G: Includes Graphic Organizer
GO: Graphic Organizer is also available 8½" x 11" online download at www.gallopade.com/client/go
(numbers above correspond to the graphic organizer numbers online)

What Is a Solar System?

Read the text, study the illustration, and answer the questions.

The universe is a vast place filled with many stars, planets, and other objects. Earth, the planet we live on, is part of a solar system. It is helpful to think of the solar system as our neighborhood in space.

Our solar system is made up of the sun, the 8 planets that revolve around it, and the moons that revolve around the planets. The solar system also includes comets, asteroids, meteoroids, and other space objects. In fact, everything that orbits around the sun is part of our solar system.

Comets consist of ice, frozen gases, and rocks. They move in long, elliptical orbits around the sun that take many years to complete. Halley's Comet is a well-known comet with one of the shortest orbits of roughly 75 years.

Asteroids are irregularly shaped rocks. Some asteroids are as large as minor planets. The Asteroid Belt, a doughnut-shaped ring of rocks, is located between Mars and Jupiter. It contains most of the asteroids in our solar system. Meteoroids are small pieces of rock and metal that travel through space.

Galaxies are much larger communities in space than solar systems. With the help of telescopes, people have observed about 170 billion galaxies! Earth and our solar system are part of the Milky Way galaxy. It is estimated that the Milky Way galaxy contains between 100 to 400 billion stars and 100 billion planets.

1. A. Use the text and illustration to infer the meaning of revolve.
   B. Use the text and illustration to infer the meaning of orbit.
   C. Are revolve and orbit synonyms or antonyms?
2. Use the text and illustration to number the following objects in order from smallest (1) to largest (5).
   __ sun __ Earth __ universe __ Milky Way galaxy __ solar system
3. Research the differences between meteoroid, meteor, and meteorite. Write a journal entry, imagining you are a meteoroid as you go through the phases of becoming a meteor and meteorite. Include illustrations.

Our Solar System

Astronomy is the branch of science that studies space and the objects in space.

Astronomers measure distances in the solar system with astronomical units (AU). An AU is the average distance between the sun and Earth, which equals 93 million miles, or nearly 150 million kilometers. Neptune is the planet furthest from the sun, about 30 AU.

4. "Astro means "related to the stars." What words in the text are formed from the root word "astro"?
5. Use information from the text to infer the meaning of astronomer.
6. A. Explain what an AU is and what it is used to measure.
   B. Why do you think scientists use AU instead of numbers?
7. Based on the information in the text, is the illustration drawn to scale? Explain how you reached your answer.
8. Experts used to include 9 planets instead of 8 in our solar system. Use online or classroom resources to research Pluto, the planet that dropped out. Why is Pluto no longer considered a planet?

Life on Earth

Read the text and answer the questions.

While you cannot feel it, Earth is moving all the time. It rotates on its axis as it orbits the sun. Earth's axis runs from the center of the North Pole to the center of the South Pole and has a tilt of 23.5 degrees.

Earth is the only planet in our solar system that is habitable, or able to support life. Earth is a safe distance from the sun. It has a protective, breathable atmosphere and temperatures comfortable for human life. Earth's atmosphere is made up of gases, mostly nitrogen and oxygen. Plants on Earth continuously give off oxygen during photosynthesis. Humans and animals need that oxygen to survive.

At the center of Earth is a dense core made of molten iron. The core sets up Earth's magnetic field, which reaches far into space and provides a magnetic covering around the planet. This covering pushes away dangerous electrically charged particles from the sun and protects us from harmful radiation. When astronauts travel outside Earth's magnetic field into space, they must be protected from the sun's dangerous radiation.

Earth is a rocky planet with a variety of terrain, including mountains, deserts, plains, and plateaus. However, about 71% of the Earth's surface is covered in water, an element essential for human survival. Over 96% of Earth's water is in the oceans.

1. A. Use a dictionary to define axis and molten as they are used in the text.
   B. What is photosynthesis? How does it support life on Earth?
2. List 4 reasons why Earth can support life.
3. Infer why Earth is blue when seen from space.
4. A. Predict what would happen to Earth's water if Earth's temperature was much colder.
   B. Predict what would happen to life on Earth if Earth's magnetic field was taken away.
5. Draw an illustration of Earth. Use a protractor to draw the axis tilted at 23.5 degrees. Mark the North and South Poles.

CAUSE AND EFFECT

Time and Space

Read the text and answer the questions.

Days, months, years, and seasons are all related to the movements of the Earth, moon, and sun. The change from day to night is caused by Earth's rotation. As our planet spins on its axis, the side of Earth that faces the sun experiences daylight, while the side that is away from the sun experiences nighttime. Earth makes one full rotation in 24 hours, or one day.

It takes Earth 365 days—one year—to orbit the sun. The four seasons of spring, summer, autumn, and winter are due to the tilt of the Earth's axis and its position around the sun. When the northern hemisphere of Earth is tilted toward the sun, it gets more sunlight and enjoys the warmth of spring and summer. At the same time, the southern half is tilted away from the sun and gets less sunlight, so it experiences the cooler temperatures of autumn and winter. Later in its orbit, Earth's tilt causes the southern hemisphere to be closer to the sun and the northern half to receive less sunlight.

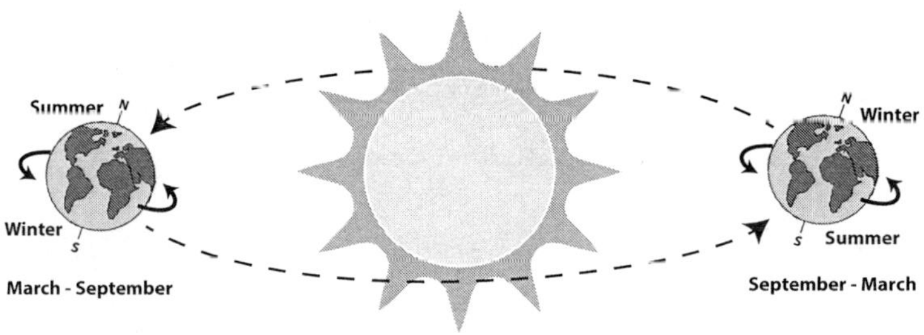

1. Is the change from day to night caused by Earth's rotation or by Earth's orbit around the sun?

2. Are Earth's seasons affected by the tilt of Earth's axis or the moon's orbit around Earth?

3. Fill in the empty Cause/Effect boxes.

Cause: Northern half of Earth tilted toward sun → **Effect:**

Cause: → **Effect:** Summer in southern hemisphere

Phases of the Moon

Read the text, study the illustration, and answer the questions.

Like Earth, the moon has a proper name, too—Luna. Unlike Earth, the moon is much smaller and does not have water or an atmosphere. One side of the moon always faces our planet, and the other side always faces away.

Throughout the month, we see different amounts of sunlight reflected on the moon, making the moon appear to have different shapes at different times. The shapes are called the phases of the moon. It takes about 29 days, called a lunar month, for the cycle to complete, going from new moon to new moon.

During a full moon, the entire moon is illuminated by sunlight. During a quarter moon, only half of the moon is lit. A gibbous moon is lit up about three-quarters of the way, while a crescent moon has only a small wedge illuminated. No sunlight is reflected towards Earth during a new moon.

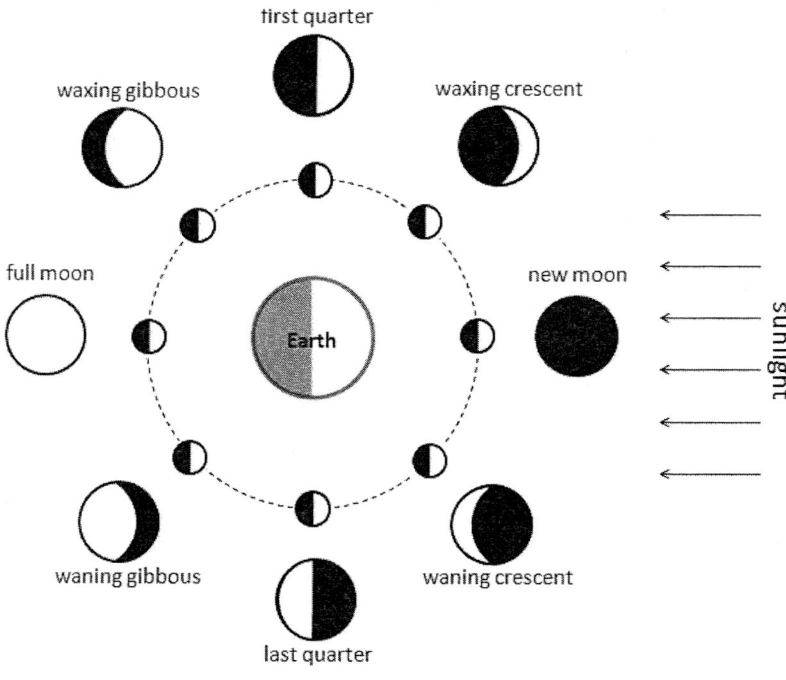

1. A. Using the text, infer the meaning of the word lunar.
   B. Use classroom and online sources to look up the etymology (word history) of Luna and lunar.
   C. Where did the name Luna originate?
2. Finish this sentence: Earth is to planet as Luna is to ________.
3. How do the phases of the moon affect how we divide up our year?
4. Waxing means "growing" and waning means "shrinking." Using that information, does the cycle of lunar phases in the illustration proceed clockwise or counterclockwise to move from a new moon to a full moon?
5. Look at the two representations of the lunar cycle, one nearer Earth, and the second further out.
   A. Which representation shows the perspective of moon phases as seen from Earth?
   B. Which representation shows the perspective of the lunar cycle as seen from a point above our solar system?
   C. Infer how the moon would look from the perspective of the sun. Would it ever be dark?
6. A. During what phase is the moon most likely to light up the night sky?
   B. During what phase will the moon be invisible in the night sky?
7. What is meant by the phrase "dark side of the moon"?
8. Use the graphic organizer to compare the similarities and differences between the moon and Earth.

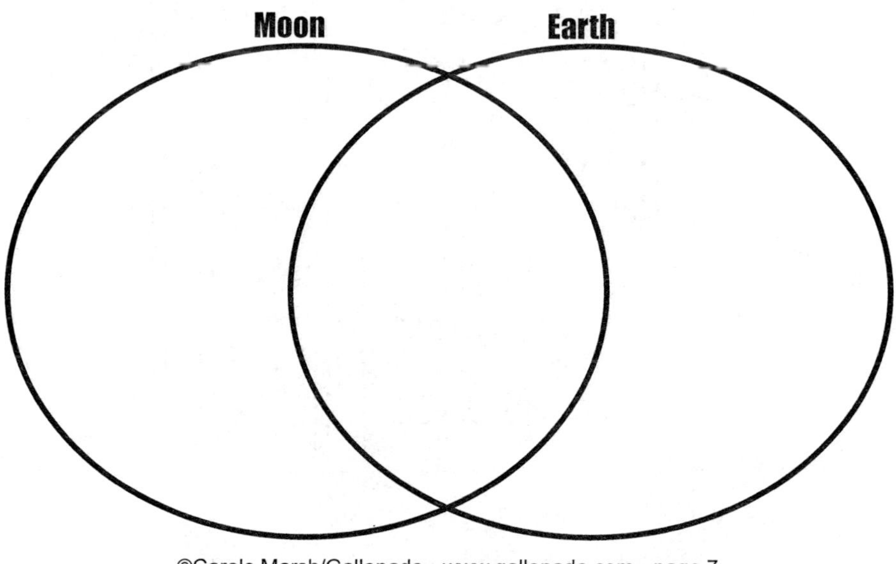

OBSERVE AND RECORD

Moon Observation Journal

Document your observations of the moon over the next five weeks. Draw how it looks each night and label the full moon, new moon, crescent moon, quarter moon, etc. Be sure to note the date you start and end your journal.

Moon Observation Chart

Start Date:

End Date:

Sunday	Monday	Tuesday	Wednesday	Thursday	Friday	Saturday

Space Quotations

Read each quotation from people who have traveled in space. Complete the chart and answer the questions.

Quotations:	What each quote means to me:
"We were flying over America and suddenly I saw snow…I have never visited America, but I imagined that the arrival of autumn and winter is the same there as in other places, and the process of getting ready for them is the same. And then it struck me that we are all children of our Earth." — Aleksandr Aleksandrov, Bulgarian cosmonaut	
"The first day or so, we all pointed to our countries. The third or fourth day, we were pointing to our continents. By the fifth day, we were aware of only one Earth." — Sultan bin Salman Al-Saud, Saudi Arabian astronaut	
"For those who have seen the Earth from space…the experience most certainly changes your perspective. The things that we share in our world are far more valuable than those which divide us." — Donald Williams, US astronaut	

1. What is the common theme shared by all three quotations?
2. Do the quotations represent objective (factual) or subjective (personal) perspectives from the astronauts and cosmonaut?
3. A. Infer the feelings that the astronauts and cosmonaut were experiencing when they viewed Earth from space.
   B. Research other quotes from astronauts about viewing Earth from space. Imagine you are an astronaut. Write a paragraph about what you see, think, and feel as you view your planet. Share your paragraph with the class.

Gravity

Read the text, study the illustration, and answer the questions.

Gravity is the force of an object that holds it together and pulls other objects toward its center. Any object that has mass has gravity, including planets, stars, moons—and you! People do not have enough mass to exert much gravitational pull on objects around them, however.

Gravitational force is increased as an object's mass increases. Earth has a lot of mass, and its gravity holds us to its surface and keeps us from floating off into space. When you drop something, it falls "down," that is, toward Earth's center. Earth's gravity also holds the atmosphere in place and the moon in orbit around Earth.

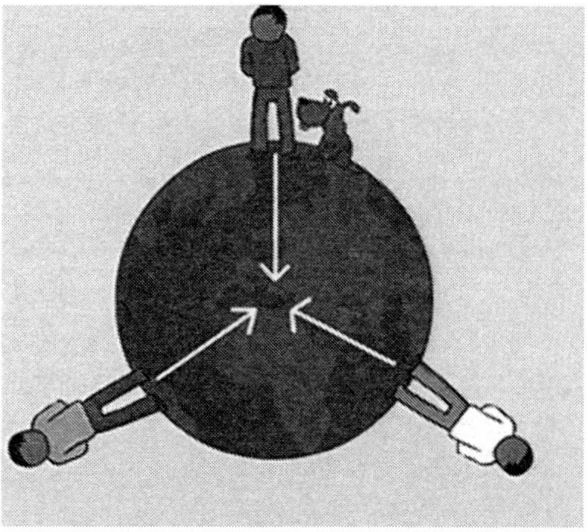

The sun is extremely massive, and its gravity is so strong that it keeps everything in our solar system, including Earth, orbiting around it. Gravitational force is also affected by how close or far an object is. Some other stars in the universe are much more massive than our sun, but they are so far away that their gravitational force does not affect us.

1. A. Use online or classroom resources to define mass as it is used in the text.
   B. Explain how Earth's mass affects its gravitational pull.
2. Use the text to explain how the illustration demonstrates gravity.
3. If an apple falls from a tree, what force pulled the apple, and what is that force pulling the apple toward?
4. If a person were standing at the equator or at the South Pole, would they fall off Earth? Why or why not?

How a Telescope Works

Read the text, study the illustration, and answer the questions.

While it is easy to see the sun, moon, bright stars, and nearby planets in our sky, objects that are deep in space are impossible to see with our eyes alone. A telescope is a tool that astronomers use to observe objects that are extremely distant.

Our eyes gather light and let us view things nearby. If an object is far away but very large, we can still see it but not with much detail because only a small image of it is projected onto the back of our eyes.

A telescope gathers a lot of light and focuses it to make an image that is small but bright. A lens is set in the eyepiece that magnifies it, so a larger image is projected. The larger image shows us details that we would not be able to see in a small image.

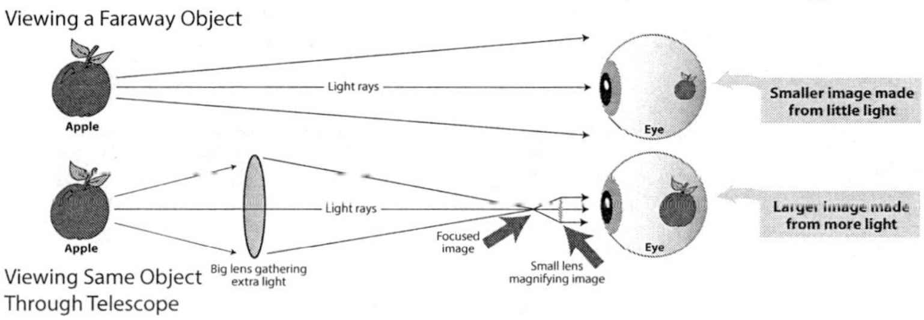

Telescopes have been in use since the early 1600s. Today, the Hubble Space Telescope orbits Earth in a satellite. It observes distant parts of the universe and sends information to scientists. You'll find some of the same technology that telescopes use in binoculars and cameras.

1. Use a dictionary to define magnifies as it is used in the text. Does magnification increase or decrease the size of an object being viewed?
2. Does a telescope require more or less light than the human eye alone to see an object in space? Use the illustration to determine your answer.
3. Explain how a telescope and binoculars are similar.
4. Divide into groups. Create a presentation on the Hubble Telescope. Include photographs the telescope has taken. Present it to the class.

CHRONOLOGICAL EVENTS

Space Exploration Timeline

Use online or classroom resources to research the events in the Word Bank. Date them and put them in chronological order, from the first event at the bottom left (1) to the most recent event at the top right (8).

Dates	Word Bank
_______	Ed White performs America's first spacewalk.
_______	NASA is formed.
_______	USSR launches Sputnik I.
_______	Neil Armstrong becomes first man to walk on the moon.
_______	John Glenn orbits Earth three times.
_______	U.S. Explorer I satellite is launched.
_______	Alan Shepard becomes first American in space.
_______	Russian Yuri Gagarin becomes first man in space.

6

5

4

3

2

1

8

7

The Sun and the Stars

Read the text, review the illustration, and answer the questions.

The sun is a star that appears larger and brighter than other stars because it is so close to us. It is the center of our solar system—the brightest, largest, and most massive object in it! In fact, more than 99% of the mass in our solar system is in the sun. It is the sun's light and energy that make life possible on Earth.

Our sun has a proper name: Sol. It is a yellow dwarf star, also known as an "average" star. Our sun may be called "average," but it is still huge. The sun is almost 110 times wider than the diameter of Earth!

Sol started out as all stars and planets do, as a nebula, a huge cloud of dust and gas. The cloud spun and its material was pulled toward the center until the sun was formed, mostly from hydrogen and helium gases. Other material in the nebula formed into the other objects in our solar system, including Earth.

Stars go through a life cycle. They are born, grow older, and eventually die. Throughout their life cycles, stars are different sizes and have different colors and forms. How a star evolves depends on its mass.

Life Cycle of a Star

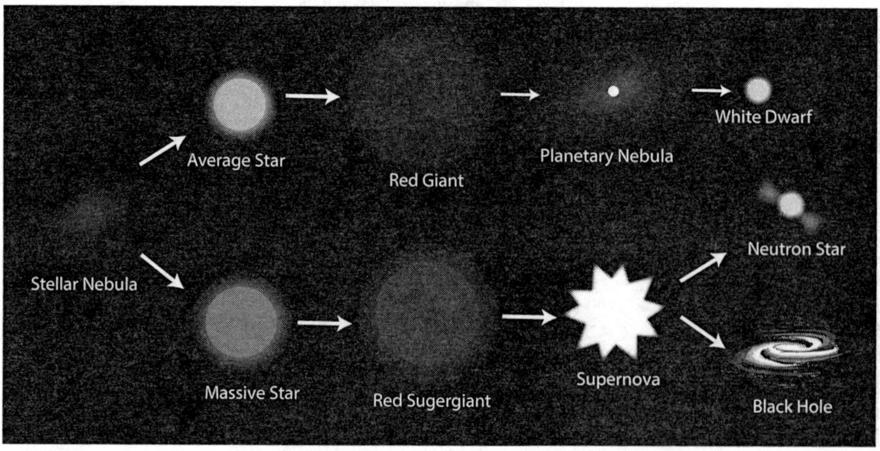

How many stars are in the universe? It is impossible to know for sure, but astronomers estimate that the number of stars is 100 octillion—that is a 1 with 29 zeros after it!

Stars range greatly in their distance from Earth. The sun is our nearest star. The average distance between the sun and Earth—1 AU or astronomical unit—is 93 million miles. It takes light from the sun about 8 minutes to travel to Earth.

A light-year is another measure of distance that astronomers use. It equals the distance that light travels in one year, and is equal to about 6 trillion miles.

Many stars are much brighter and larger than Sol, but are so far away that they appear as dots of light in our night sky. The next nearest star to Earth is Proxima Centauri. It is 4.2 light-years from the sun.

Have you ever wondered why you can't see stars during the daytime? The reason is the sun's bright light overwhelms the light from stars. But at night, when the part of the Earth where you live is not facing the sun, you can see the light coming from the stars.

1. Why does the sun appear brighter to us than any other star?
2. Predict what life would be like on Earth without the energy and light that comes from the sun.
3. A. Which part of the illustration shows the life cycle of our sun? How do you know?
   B. Is our sun one of the largest stars in the universe? How do you know?
   C. What is the next stage for our sun's life cycle?
4. A. Use the text to define light-year.
   B. Does a light-year refer to a measure of time or distance?
5. How long does it take for light from Proxima Centauri to reach Earth? How did you reach your answer?
6. Though it looks like the sun is a solid, yellow ball, there is actually a lot of activity on the sun. Use classroom and online resources to research and define solar flares and sunspots. Find photos to go with your definitions and display them on posterboard.

PRIMARY SOURCE ANALYSIS

Poetry of the Stars

Read the poem and text and answer the questions.

Winter Stars
By Sara Teasdale

I went out at night alone;
The young blood flowing beyond the sea
Seemed to have drenched my spirit's wings—
I bore my sorrow heavily.

But when I lifted up my head
From shadows shaken on the snow,
I saw Orion in the east
Burn steadily as long ago.

From windows in my father's house,
Dreaming my dreams on winter nights,
I watched Orion as a girl
Above another city's lights.

Years go, dreams go, and youth goes too,
The world's heart breaks beneath its wars,
All things are changed, save in the east
The faithful beauty of the stars.

Sara Teasdale (1884-1933) was an award-winning American poet who was born in Missouri and later lived in New York City.

1. What is the tone of this poem? Is it hopeful, discouraging, or both?
2. What world war occurred during the poet's life that might be referenced by the second line?
3. A. What is Orion? Use online or classroom resources to find out.
   B. Where did the author watch Orion as a young girl?
   C. Where was the author when she watched Orion as an adult?
4. What point is the author making about the meaning of Orion and the stars in her life? Discuss as a class.

Solar and Lunar Eclipses

Read the text and answer the questions.

Our perspective from Earth gives us many spectacular views of space events. Solar and lunar eclipses are two of these events.

A solar eclipse occurs when the moon's orbit brings it between Earth and the sun. The moon blocks all or part of the sunlight from reaching Earth.

A lunar eclipse occurs when the Earth passes between the sun and the moon. The Earth blocks sunlight from reaching the moon. Eclipses do not happen often because the moon is usually too high or low in its orbit to block the sun or catch the Earth's shadow.

Illustration A

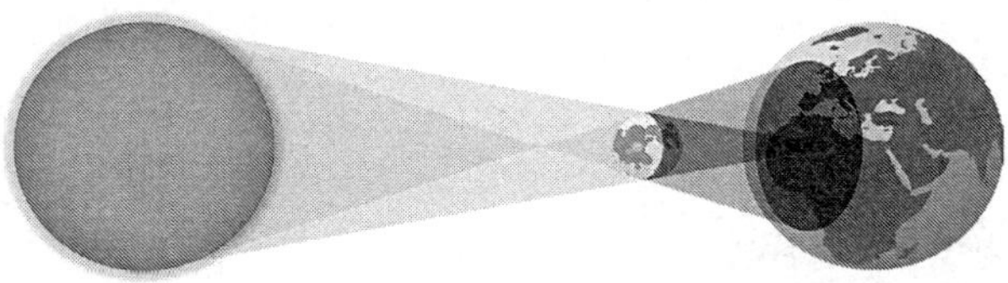

Illustration B

1. A. Based on the text, does Illustration A show a lunar or solar eclipse?
   B. Research and draw how the sun looks to people on Earth when the moon blocks it.
2. A. Based on the text, does Illustration B show a lunar or solar eclipse?
   B. Research and draw how the moon looks to people on Earth when Earth's shadow blocks the sunlight.
3. Do all people on Earth see exactly the same thing when an eclipse occurs? How do you know?

Planets in Our Solar System

Read the text and answer the questions.

There are 8 planets in our solar system. They are divided into two groups—the Inner Planets and the Outer Planets.

The Inner Planets are closer to the sun. They are known as "Terrestrial Planets" because they are small and dense with rocky compositions. Earth is the only planet suited for life as we know it.

Mercury—closest to the sun; smallest planet; rocky with craters, no water; very thin atmosphere of hydrogen, helium, oxygen; temperatures range from 800°F to -290°F; no moon

Venus—second from the sun; sixth largest planet; surface rocky with mountains, no liquid water; thick atmosphere of carbon dioxide and nitrogen; temperatures reach 900°F; no moon

Earth—third from the sun; fifth largest planet; surface is 30% landmasses, 70% water; atmosphere is a thick layer of breathable nitrogen and oxygen; average temperature near 60°F; 1 moon

Mars—fourth from the sun; seventh largest planet; surface is rocky with deserts, no water; atmosphere is thin layer of carbon dioxide; average temperature -67°F; 2 moons

The Outer Planets are located beyond the Asteroid Belt and are very large. They are also known as "Gas Giants" since they have no clear, solid surfaces, and their atmospheres are made up of gases, mostly hydrogen and helium. All of the Outer Planets have many moons, as well as rings of dust, ice, or rocks that orbit them.

Jupiter—fifth from the sun; largest of all planets; average temperature is about -234°F; 67 moons

Saturn—sixth from the sun; second largest planet; average temperature is about -288°F; 62 moons, 7 shining rings

Uranus—seventh from the sun; third largest planet; average temperature is about -350°F, called an "Ice Giant"; 27 moons

Neptune—eighth from the sun; fourth largest planet; average temperature is about -350°F, called an "Ice Giant"; 14 moons

1. What are the other names for the Inner and Outer Planets? Explain why those names were chosen.
2. Name 3 things the Outer Planets have in common.
3. Fill in the table with information from the text. Put a circle around the name of each Inner Planet, and a box around the name of each Outer Planet.

Planet	Surface	Atmosphere	Temperature
Mercury			
Venus			
Earth			
Mars			
Jupiter			
Saturn			
Uranus			
Neptune			

PRIMARY SOURCE ANALYSIS

Lunar Module Plaque

Answer the questions using the text and photograph.

In July 1969, America's Apollo 11 spacecraft landed on the moon. It was the first manned space mission where men actually landed on the moon and walked on the moon's surface. A stainless steel plaque was attached to the ladder of the lunar module and remained permanently on the moon. A replica of the plaque is shown in the photograph.

Courtesy of NASA

1. Use a dictionary to define plaque and replica as they are used in the text. List a synonym for each word.
2. In your opinion, why did NASA decide to leave this plaque behind on the moon?
3. Why do you think the plaque includes two views of Earth?
4. Do you think it is important that the plaque says, "We came in peace for all mankind"? Why or why not? Discuss as a class.

Space Science Vocabulary

Use a dictionary and other resources to complete the graphic organizer for each vocabulary word.

asteroid	constellation	star
comet	orbit	atmosphere
meteor	astronomy	galaxy
astronaut	eclipse	telescope

Word	Definition
Use It in a Sentence	

COMPARE PRIMARY SOURCES

Space Program Points of View

Read the excerpts from the primary sources and answer the questions.

In 1962, President John F. Kennedy presented a speech to 35,000 people in Houston, Texas, explaining why mankind should explore the moon.

> "...Those who came before us made certain that this country rode the first waves of the industrial revolutions, the first waves of modern invention, and the first wave of nuclear power, and this generation does not intend to founder in the backwash of the coming age of space. We mean to be a part of it—we mean to lead it. For the eyes of the world now look into space, to the moon and to the planets beyond, and we have vowed that we shall not see it governed by a hostile flag of conquest, but by a banner of freedom and peace. We have vowed that we shall not see space filled with weapons of mass destruction, but with instruments of knowledge and understanding. Yet the vows of this Nation can only be fulfilled if we in this Nation are first, and, therefore, we intend to be first...
>
> "...We set sail on this new sea because there is new knowledge to be gained, and new rights to be won, and they must be won and used for the progress of all people. For space science, like nuclear science and all technology, has no conscience of its own. Whether it will become a force for good or ill depends on man, and only if the United States occupies a position of pre-eminence can we help decide whether this new ocean will be a sea of peace or a new terrifying theater of war...
>
> "...And, therefore, as we set sail we ask God's blessing on the most hazardous and dangerous and greatest adventure on which man has ever embarked."

1. List 2 reasons that President Kennedy believed it was important for U.S. astronauts to go to the moon.
2. According to President Kennedy, what important thing will be assured if the United States is the strongest presence in space exploration?
3. What is the "greatest adventure" that the president is referring to in the last paragraph?

Many African-American newspapers questioned the wisdom of American funds going to space research at a time when many people, especially African-Americans, were struggling economically. The *Los Angeles Sentinel* ran an editorial in 1969 that argued against the Apollo space mission and summed up the concerns of many Americans.

> "...Does the fact that we are preparing for space travel <u>circumvent</u> the fact that hunger and strife still exist unabated in this wonderful country of plenty?...
>
> "Does the millions of dollars spent on space programs supplement the millions needed to feed the starving people in the black ghettos across the nation? Will the flight to the moon find adequate housing for those people...?
>
> "...It would appear that the fathers of our nation would allow a few thousand hungry people to die for the lack of a few thousand dollars while they would contaminate the moon and its sterility for the sake of 'progress' and spend billions of dollars in the process, while people are hungry, ill-clothed, poorly educated (if at all)."

4. Use a dictionary to define <u>circumvent</u> as it is used in the text. List several synonyms.
5. A. The editorial above was published in 1969. Use online or classroom resources to find out what important event in space exploration occurred in that year.
   B. In your research, find out how most Americans viewed the space program at that time. Did the majority of Americans support it?
6. A. Summarize the main idea of President Kennedy's speech excerpts.
   B. Summarize the main idea of the excerpts from the editorial.
   C. Compare and contrast the two viewpoints.
7. Which viewpoint do you agree with? Write a paragraph explaining your opinion. Use facts to support it. Proofread and edit your work. Discuss your opinions as a class.
8. Space exploration has provided many new products and technologies to people around the world. Research the benefits that have come from space travel and exploration. Create a computer presentation with photographs and text.

Correlations to Common Core State Standards

For your convenience, correlations are listed page-by-page and for the entire book!

This book is correlated to the Common Core State Standards for English Language Arts grades 3-8, and to Common Core State Standards for Literacy in History, Science, & Technological Subjects grades 6-8.

Correlations are highlighted in gray.

PAGE #	READING *Includes:* RI: Reading Informational Text RH: Reading History	WRITING *Includes:* W: Writing WHST: Writing History, Science, & Technology	LANGUAGE *Includes:* L: Language LF: Language Foundational Skills	SPEAKING & LISTENING *Includes:* SL: Speaking & Listening
2-3	RI/RH . **1** 2 **3** **4** **5** 6 **7** 8 9 **10**	W/WHST . 1 **2** **3** **4** 5 6 **7** 8 **9** **10**	L/LF . 1 2 3 **4** **5** **6**	SL . 1 2 3 4 5 6
4	RI/RH . **1** 2 **3** **4** 5 6 7 8 9 **10**	W/WHST . 1 **2** 3 **4** 5 6 7 8 9 **10**	L/LF . 1 2 3 **4** 5 **6**	SL . 1 2 3 4 5 6
5	RI/RH . **1** 2 **3** 4 **5** 6 **7** **8** 9 **10**	W/WHST . 1 2 3 **4** 5 6 7 8 9 10	L/LF . 1 2 3 4 5 6	SL . 1 2 3 4 5 6
6-7	RI/RH . **1** 2 **3** **4** **5** 6 **7** **8** 9 **10**	W/WHST . 1 **2** 3 **4** 5 6 7 8 9 **10**	L/LF . 1 2 3 **4** **5** **6**	SL . 1 2 3 4 5 6
8	RI/RH . 1 2 3 **4** 5 6 **7** 8 9 **10**	W/WHST . 1 2 3 4 5 6 **7** **8** 9 10	L/LF . 1 2 3 4 5 6	SL . 1 2 3 4 5 6
9	RI/RH . **1** **2** 3 4 5 6 7 **8** **9** **10**	W/WHST . **1** **2** **3** **4** 5 6 **7** 8 **9** **10**	L/LF . 1 2 3 4 **5** **6**	SL . 1 **2** 3 **4** 5 6
10	RI/RH . **1** 2 **3** **4** 5 6 **7** 8 9 **10**	W/WHST . 1 **2** 3 **4** 5 6 7 8 **9** **10**	L/LF . 1 2 3 **4** 5 **6**	SL . 1 2 3 4 5 6
11	RI/RH . **1** 2 **3** **4** 5 6 **7** 8 9 **10**	W/WHST . 1 **2** 3 **4** 5 **6** **7** 8 9 **10**	L/LF . 1 2 3 **4** 5 **6**	SL . **1** 2 3 **4** **5** **6**
12-13	RI/RH . 1 2 3 4 **5** 6 **7** 8 9 **10**	W/WHST . 1 2 3 4 5 6 **7** 8 9 10	L/LF . 1 2 3 4 5 6	SL . 1 2 3 4 5 6
14-15	RI/RH . **1** 2 **3** **4** **5** 6 **7** 8 9 **10**	W/WHST . 1 2 **3** **4** 5 6 **7** 8 9 **10**	L/LF . 1 2 3 **4** 5 **6**	SL . 1 2 3 4 5 6
16	RI/RH . **1** 2 3 4 5 6 7 **8** **9** **10**	W/WHST . **1** **2** 3 **4** 5 6 **7** 8 **9** **10**	L/LF . 1 2 3 4 **5** **6**	SL . **1** **2** 3 **4** 5 **6**
17	RI/RH . **1** 2 **3** 4 **5** 6 **7** 8 9 **10**	W/WHST . 1 **2** 3 **4** 5 6 **7** 8 **9** **10**	L/LF . 1 2 3 **4** 5 **6**	SL . 1 2 3 4 5 6
18-19	RI/RH . **1** 2 3 **4** 5 6 **7** 8 9 **10**	W/WHST . 1 **2** 3 **4** 5 6 7 8 **9** **10**	L/LF . 1 2 3 **4** 5 6	SL . 1 2 3 4 5 6
20	RI/RH . **1** 2 **3** **4** 5 **6** **7** 8 9 **10**	W/WHST . **1** **2** 3 **4** 5 6 7 8 9 **10**	L/LF . 1 2 3 **4** 5 **6**	SL . **1** 2 3 **4** 5 **6**
21	RI/RH . 1 2 3 **4** 5 6 7 8 9 **10**	W/WHST . 1 2 3 **4** 5 6 7 8 9 10	L/LF . 1 2 3 **4** 5 **6**	SL . 1 2 3 4 5 6
22-23	RI/RH . **1** **2** **3** **4** **5** 6 7 **8** **9** **10**	W/WHST . **1** **2** 3 **4** **5** **6** **7** **8** **9** **10**	L/LF . 1 2 3 **4** 5 **6**	SL . **1** **2** 3 **4** **5** **6**
COMPLETE BOOK	RI/RH . **1** **2** **3** **4** **5** **6** **7** **8** **9** **10**	W/WHST . **1** **2** **3** **4** **5** **6** **7** **8** **9** **10**	L/LF . 1 2 3 **4** **5** **6**	SL . **1** **2** 3 **4** **5** **6**

For the complete Common Core standard identifier, combine your grade + "." + letter code above + "." + number code above.

In addition to the correlations indicated here, the activities may be adapted or expanded to align to additional standards and to meet the diverse needs of your unique students!